healthy family
recipes

Published by:
TRIDENT REFERENCE PUBLISHING
801 12th Avenue South, Suite 400
Naples, Fl 34102 USA

Tel: + 1 (239) 649-7077
www.tridentreference.com
email: sales@tridentreference.com

healthy family
recipes

Healthy Family Recipes
© TRIDENT REFERENCE PUBLISHING

Publisher
Simon St. John Bailey

Editor-in-chief
Susan Knightley

Prepress
Precision Prep & Press

Includes Index
ISBN 1582797358
UPC 6 15269 97358 5

Printed in The United States

introduction

Gone are the days when healthy eating meant boring food. Today there is an awareness of the need to develop eating habits that include foods which are lower in fat, sugar and salt and higher in dietary fiber. But no one wants to eat food that is tasteless.

This book makes the most of fresh ingredients to create delicious dishes that

healthy family recipes
introduction

will be enjoyed by the whole family... and by all who care to try them. Even if you are a weight watcher or a vegetarian, there will be many recipes of interest to you.

With the multitude of food "scares" that regularly appear in the media, feeding the family has become a source of concern for many people. If you are one of them, stop worrying. Here is the proof that healthy eating and good food can go hand in hand. We have endeavored to present you with attractive recipes consisting of everyday wholesome and natural ingredients, prepared and cooked in the most simple manner.

Vegetables, fruit, low fat dairy products, cereal and grain foods such as pasta, rice, bread, polenta, couscous and flour are all high in fiber and low in fat. For healthy cooking, use them as the main ingredients, include reasonable quantities of fish, lean meat or chicken without the skin and add very little oil, butter or margarine.

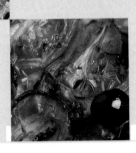

However, it should be remembered that not everything you eat will be low in fat and high in fiber –the secret to a healthy eating plan is to balance what you eat.

Nutritional guidelines

- Excess fat is the major nutrition problem in most Western countries. However, total avoidance of fat is not desirable. A small amount is required to provide fat-soluble vitamins A, D, E and K.
- A healthy diet should include a range of foods rich in both insoluble and soluble fiber to help with bowel regularity and lowering of cholesterol levels.
- Carbohydrates are the body's preferred source of energy. Bread, pasta and rice are excellent forms of complex carbohydrates.
- Most people need to cut down on salt as a high salt intake rises blood pressure. Do not salt food for your baby or children.
- Sugar supplies no other nutrients than carbohydrates and can be eliminated from the family diet without harm.

Difficulty scale

■□□I Easy to do

■■□I Requires attention

■■■I Requires experience

pasta
with rocket pesto

■ □ □ | Cooking time: 15 minutes - Preparation time: 5 minutes

ingredients

> **500 g/1 lb fettuccine**
> **Parmesan cheese shavings**

rocket pesto

> **250 g/8 oz rocket**
> **60 g/2 oz pine nuts**
> **30 g/1 oz Parmesan cheese, grated**
> **2 cloves garlic, crushed**
> **3 tablespoons olive oil**

method

1. Cook pasta in boiling water in a large saucepan following packet directions. Drain, set aside and keep warm.
2. To make pesto, place rocket, pine nuts, Parmesan cheese and garlic in a food processor or blender and process to finely chop. With machine running, slowly add oil and process until smooth.
3. Add pesto to hot pasta and toss to combine. Serve topped with Parmesan cheese shavings.

....
Serves 4

tip from the chef

Serve this tasty pasta dish with a light sauté. To make sauté, place a tablespoon of olive oil in a frying pan. Add 1 sliced onion and 1 tablespoon minced garlic and cook over a medium heat until soft. Add 1 chopped eggplant and 2 sliced green peppers and cook, stirring frequently, for 5 minutes. Add 440 g/14 oz canned tomatoes and cook, stirring occasionally, for 10-15 minutes longer or until eggplant is soft.

spaghetti
bolognese

I☐☐ I Cooking time: 45 minutes - Preparation time: 10 minutes

method

1. Cook spaghetti in boiling water in a large saucepan following packet directions. Drain, set aside and keep warm.
2. To make sauce, heat oil in a frying pan over a medium heat, add onion and garlic and cook, stirring, for 3 minutes or until onion is golden. Add beef and mushrooms and cook, stirring, for 5 minutes longer or until beef is brown. Drain off excess fat.
3. Stir tomatoes, wine, tomato paste (purée) and Worcestershire sauce into pan and bring to the boil. Reduce heat and simmer, stirring occasionally, for 25 minutes or until mixture reduces and thickens.
4. Spoon sauce over spaghetti, sprinkle with parsley and Parmesan cheese and serve.

Serves 4

ingredients

> 500 g/1 lb wholemeal spaghetti
> 2 tablespoons chopped fresh parsley
> 60 g/2 oz Parmesan cheese, grated

bolognese sauce

> 1 tablespoon olive oil
> 1 onion, chopped
> 1 clove garlic, crushed
> 300 g/10 oz lean beef mince
> 125 g/4 oz button mushrooms, sliced
> 440 g/14 oz canned tomatoes, drained and mashed
> 1/4 cup/60 ml/2 fl oz red wine
> 2 tablespoons tomato paste (purée)
> 1 tablespoon Worcestershire sauce

tip from the chef

Other pastas such as penne, fettuccine and pappardelle are also good choices for this ever popular dish. Choose wholemeal varieties for added fiber.

creamy tomato tortellini

■□□ | Cooking time: 15 minutes - Preparation time: 5 minutes

ingredients
> **500 g/1 lb tortellini**

creamy tomato sauce
> **2 teaspoons vegetable oil**
> **1 clove garlic, crushed**
> **4 spring onions, chopped**
> **4 rashers bacon, chopped**
> **440 g/14 oz canned tomatoes, chopped**
> **1 tablespoon chopped fresh rosemary or 1/2 teaspoon dried rosemary**
> **1 cup/250 ml/8 fl oz light cream**

method
1. Cook pasta in boiling water in a large saucepan following packet directions. Drain, set aside and keep warm.
2. To make sauce, heat oil in a frying pan over a medium heat, add garlic, spring onions and bacon and cook, stirring, for 3 minutes or until bacon is crispy.
3. Stir in tomatoes, rosemary and cream, bring to simmering and simmer for 3 minutes or until heated through. Add hot pasta and toss to combine.

....
Serves 4

tip from the chef
If you have a good supply of garlic, chop a large quantity in the food processor when you have time to spare. To store, place chopped garlic in a screwtop jar, pour over enough olive oil to cover, seal and store in the refrigerator. The garlic will keep for about a month.

vegetable
lasagna

■ ■ □ | Cooking time: 50 minutes - Preparation time: 15 minutes

method

1. Heat a large nonstick frying pan over a medium-high heat, add broccoli, cauliflower, beans, red pepper, zucchini. carrots, tomato purée, parsley and chili sauce, bring to simmering and simmer for 5-8 minutes or until vegetables are tender. Remove pan from heat and set aside.

2. To make sauce, place milk in a saucepan and heat over a medium heat, stirring occasionally, for 4-5 minutes or until almost boiling. Stir in cornflour mixture and cook, stirring constantly, for 3-4 minutes or until sauce boils and thickens. Stir in mustard and season to taste with black pepper.

3. Line an ovenproof dish with 4 lasagna sheets, top with one-third of the vegetable mixture and one-third of the sauce. Repeat layers, finishing with sauce. Combine Parmesan and Cheddar cheeses, sprinkle over top of lasagna and bake at 180°C/350°F/Gas 4 for 30 minutes or until lasagna sheets are soft.

Serves 4

ingredients

- > **250 g/8 oz broccoli flowerets**
- > **250 g/8 oz cauliflower flowerets**
- > **125 g/4 oz green beans, sliced**
- > **1 red pepper, chopped**
- > **2 zucchini, sliced**
- > **2 carrots, sliced**
- > **440 g/14 oz tomato purée**
- > **2 tablespoons chopped fresh parsley**
- > **2 teaspoons chili sauce**
- > **12 sheets instant spinach lasagna**
- > **45 g/1 1/2 oz Parmesan cheese, grated**
- > **45 g/1 1/2 oz Cheddar cheese, grated**

white sauce

- > **2 cups/500 ml/16 fl oz milk**
- > **2 tablespoons cornflour blended with 3 tablespoons water**
- > **1 teaspoon Dijon mustard**
- > **freshly ground black pepper**

tip from the chef

If you wish to reduce even more the fat content of this dish, use skim milk and replace Parmesan and Cheddar cheeses for low fat mozzarella cheese.

pumpkin and artichoke risotto

■□□ | Cooking time: 35 minutes - Preparation time: 15 minutes

method

1. Place stock and wine in a saucepan and bring to the boil over a medium heat. Reduce heat and keep warm.
2. Heat oil in a saucepan over a medium heat, add onion, cumin and nutmeg and cook, stirring, for 3 minutes or until onion is soft. Add pumpkin and cook, stirring, for 3 minutes.
3. Add rice and cook, stirring, for 5 minutes. Pour 1 cup/250 ml/8 fl oz hot stock mixture into rice and cook over a medium heat, stirring constantly, until stock is absorbed. Continue cooking in this way until all the stock is used and rice is tender.
4. Add artichokes, sun-dried tomatoes, sage and black pepper to taste to rice mixture. Mix gently and cook for 2 minutes or until heated through. Remove pan from heat, gently stir in Parmesan cheese and serve.

Serves 4

ingredients

> 3 cups/750 ml/1¼ pt vegetable stock
> 1 cup/250 ml/8 fl oz white wine
> 1 tablespoon olive oil
> 1 onion, chopped
> 2 teaspoons ground cumin
> ½ teaspoon ground nutmeg
> 185 g/6 oz pumpkin, chopped
> 1½ cups/330 g/11 oz arborio rice
> 440 g/14 oz canned artichoke hearts, drained and chopped
> 90 g/3 oz sun-dried tomatoes, chopped
> 2 tablespoons chopped fresh sage
> freshly ground black pepper
> 30 g/1 oz grated Parmesan cheese

tip from the chef

Arborio rice is traditionally used for making risottos. It absorbs liquid without becoming soft and it is this special quality that makes it so suitable for risottos. A risotto made in the traditional way, where liquid is added gradually as the rice cooks, takes 20-30 minutes to cook.

risotto
with green vegetables

■□□ | Cooking time: 25 minutes - Preparation time: 10 minutes

ingredients

> **1 tablespoon oil**
> **1 small onion, chopped**
> **²/₃ cup rice**
> **¹/₄ cup dry white wine**
> **1¹/₂ cups water**
> **2 tablespoons chopped fresh parsley**
> **¹/₂ cup broccoli flowerets, blanched**
> **¹/₂ cup chopped asparagus, blanched**
> **¹/₂ cup green peas, blanched**

method

1. Heat oil in a large frying pan, add onion and cook for 3 minutes. Stir in rice and wine, cook until wine is absorbed.
2. Add water, bring to the boil, cover and cook rice until tender and liquid is absorbed, approximately 20 minutes.
3. Stir vegetables into rice and serve immediately.

....
Serves 4

tip from the chef

Risotto will become more creamy and tasty if a spoonful of butter and another of grated Parmesan cheese are added before the end of cooking.

couscous pilaf

■□□ I Cooking time: 10 minutes - Preparation time: 5 minutes

method

1. In a large, deep frying pan melt the butter over moderate heat. Add onion and carrot, cook for 3 minutes.
2. Add couscous, peas, almonds and stock to pan. Simmer for 5 minutes, stirring with a fork.
3. Sprinkle extra butter over the mixture, fluff with a fork to break up any lumps. Serve warm.

....
Serves 4

ingredients

> **3 tablespoons butter**
> **1 onion, finely chopped**
> **1 large carrot, chopped**
> **200 g/6^1/$_2$ oz couscous**
> **200 g/6^1/$_2$ oz frozen peas, thawed**
> **75 g/2^1/$_2$ oz almonds, blanched, toasted**
> **1 cup chicken stock**
> **100 g/3^1/$_2$ oz butter, extra, cut into small cubes**

tip from the chef
This dish is outstanding for its high energetic quality and it is a good accompaniment to lean meats of any type.

asparagus
rice tart

■■□ | Cooking time: 70 minutes - Preparation time: 15 minutes

ingredients

rice crust

> 1 cup/220 g/7 oz brown rice, cooked
> 125 g/4 oz tasty cheese (mature Cheddar), grated
> 30 g/1 oz butter, melted
> 2 tablespoons snipped fresh chives
> 2 eggs, lightly beaten

asparagus filling

> 1 tablespoon vegetable oil
> 2 onions, chopped
> 440 g/14 oz asparagus spears, cut into 5 cm/2 in pieces
> 1 red pepper, sliced
> 125 g/4 oz snow peas, sliced
> 5 eggs, lightly beaten
> 1 cup/250 g/8 oz sour cream
> 30 g/1 oz Parmesan cheese, grated
> freshly ground black pepper

method

1. To make crust, place rice, cheese, butter, chives and eggs (a) in a bowl and mix well to combine. Press mixture over the base and up the sides of a greased deep-sided 23 cm/9 in flan tin. Set aside.

2. To make filling, heat oil in a frying pan over a medium heat, add onions and cook, stirring, for 5 minutes or until soft and golden. Add asparagus, red pepper and snow peas and cook for 3 minutes longer. Remove pan from heat and set aside to cool completely.

3. Place eggs, sour cream, Parmesan cheese and black pepper to taste in a bowl and mix to combine. Stir in asparagus mixture (b).

4. Pour filling into rice crust (c) and bake at 160°C/325°F/Gas 3 for 1 hour or until filling is set.

....
Serves 4-6

tip from the chef

Toasted sesame seeds make a deliciously nutty addition to the rice crust. When fresh asparagus is unavailable, use another green vegetable such as broccoli, Brussels sprouts or green beans.

tomato tart

■□□ I Cooking time: 50 minutes - Preparation time: 15 minutes

method

1. Place tomato halves on a wire rack set in a baking dish and bake at 200°C/400°F/ Gas 6 for 30 minutes or until soft.
2. Layer filo pastry brushing between every second layer with oil. Place layered pastry in a nonstick 18 x 28 cm/7 x 11 in shallow cake tin, trim off excess and roll edges to form a rim.
3. Spread surface of pastry with mustard, sprinkle with Parmesan cheese and top with tomatoes. Place remaining oil, parsley, garlic, thyme, oregano and black pepper to taste in a bowl and toss to combine.
4. Sprinkle oil mixture over tomatoes, scatter with olives and bake for 15-20 minutes or until pastry is golden. Serve hot, warm or at room temperature.

....
Serves 6

ingredients

> **1 kg/2 lb small tomatoes, halved**
> **8 sheets filo pastry**
> **1/4 cup/60 ml/2 fl oz olive oil**
> **1 tablespoon Dijon mustard**
> **60 g/2 oz Parmesan cheese, grated**
> **2 tablespoons chopped fresh parsley**
> **1 clove garlic, crushed**
> **1 teaspoon chopped fresh thyme or 1/2 teaspoon dried thyme**
> **1 teaspoon chopped fresh oregano or 1/2 teaspoon dried oregano**
> **freshly ground black pepper**
> **60 g/2 oz black olives, chopped**

tip from the chef

This tart is delicious accompanied by a salad as a starter. The ideal tomatoes to use for this tart are Italian ones.

all-time
vegetable pie

■□□ | Cooking time: 1 hour - Preparation time: 20 minutes

ingredients

> **125 g/4 oz tasty cheese (mature Cheddar), grated**
> **1 cup/60 g/2 oz breadcrumbs, made from stale bread**

pastry

> **1¹/2 cups/185 g/6 oz flour**
> **90 g/3 oz butter**
> **1 egg, lightly beaten**
> **1-2 tablespoons iced water**

vegetable filling

> **1 tablespoon vegetable oil**
> **1 onion, sliced**
> **2 leeks, sliced**
> **250 g/8 oz pumpkin flesh, chopped**
> **2 potatoes, chopped**
> **¹/4 cauliflower, broken into small flowerets**
> **1 parsnip, chopped**
> **1 small broccoli, broken into small flowerets**
> **1 red pepper, chopped**
> **125 g/4 oz frozen peas**
> **¹/2 cup/125 ml/4 fl oz vegetable stock**
> **2 tablespoons chopped fresh basil**

method

1. To make pastry, process flour and butter until mixture resembles breadcrumbs. Add egg and water, form a soft dough, knead briefly. Wrap in plastic wrap and chill 30 minutes. Roll out pastry to fit a deep 23 cm/9 in flan tin with a removable base. Line with nonstick paper, fill with uncooked rice and bake at 180°C/350°F/Gas 4 for 10 minutes. Remove rice and paper and bake for 10 minutes longer or until golden. Cool.

2. To make filling, heat oil in a large frying pan over a medium heat, add onion and leeks and cook, stirring, for 4 minutes or until golden. Add pumpkin and potatoes and cook, stirring, for 10 minutes longer or until just tender. Add cauliflower, parsnip, broccoli, red pepper, peas and stock and bring to the boil. Reduce heat and simmer for 10 minutes or until vegetables are soft. Mix in basil. Cool.

3. Spoon filling into pastry case. Combine cheese and breadcrumbs, sprinkle over filling and bake for 20 minutes or until top is golden.

....
Serves 6

tip from the chef
If preferred, use wholemeal plain flour to prepare a pastry with a nuttier flavor.

celery and green pepper flan

■□□ I Cooking time: 55 minutes - Preparation time: 10 minutes

method

1. Roll out pastry to fit a greased 20 cm/8 in flan tin, bake blind for 10 minutes in a moderately hot oven.
2. Heat milk in a medium saucepan over moderate heat. Add onion and bring to the boil. Strain milk and set aside.
3. Heat oil in a large saucepan over low heat, add celery, green pepper and spring onions and cook for 5 minutes. Add flour (a) and cook for 1 minute, stirring constantly. Pour in reserved milk, mix well and bring to the boil. Remove from heat, cool to room temperature. Beat in egg (b), egg whites and black pepper.
4. Pour mixture into pastry case (c) and cook for 35 minutes in a moderate oven.

....
Serves 6

ingredients

> **1 sheet shortcrust pastry**
> **1³/4 cups milk**
> **1 onion, chopped**
> **1 tablespoon oil**
> **6 stalks celery, chopped**
> **1 green pepper, seeded and chopped**
> **2 tablespoon finely chopped spring onions**
> **1¹/2 tablespoons plain flour**
> **1 egg**
> **2 egg whites**
> **¹/2 teaspoon cracked black pepper**

tip from the chef
A homemade tomato sauce will enhance the flavor of this delicious flan.

a b c

spinach
and cheese pie

■■□ | Cooking time: 45 minutes - Preparation time: 15 minutes

ingredients
> 3 tablespoons olive oil
> 1 onion, finely chopped
> 2 cups cooked spinach
> 200 g/6¹/2 oz feta cheese
> 200 g/6¹/2 oz ricotta cheese
> 4 eggs, lightly beaten
> 2 tablespoons grated Parmesan cheese
> pinch ground nutmeg
> ¹/2 cup/125 ml/4 fl oz milk
> freshly ground black pepper
> 10 sheets filo pastry

method
1. In a small frying pan, heat 1 tablespoon oil, add onion and cook until tender. Add spinach and mix well.
2. Mash feta cheese and ricotta cheese with a fork, add eggs, Parmesan cheese, spinach mixture, nutmeg, milk and pepper, stir well.
3. Brush a square tin with oil. Place 5 sheets of filo pastry at the bottom, one on top of another; brush each sheet with oil and let the edges come up the sides of the tin.
4. Spread filling evenly over pastry, fold over edges and cover with the remaining 5 sheets of pastry, tucking the edges down the sides of the tin. Brush each sheet, and the top one, with oil.
5. Cut the pie into squares with a sharp knife, but do not cut through to the bottom or the filling will leak into the pan.
6. Bake in a moderate oven about 40 minutes or until the pie is crisp, golden and puffed. Cut the squares through to the bottom and serve hot.

....
Serves 8

tip from the chef
For something different use 200 g/6¹/2 oz canned, drained salmon or tuna in brine or springwater in place of the ricotta cheese.

summer
vegetable pie

■□□ | Cooking time: 50 minutes - Preparation time: 10 minutes

method

1. Roll out pastry to fit a 25 cm/10 in flan tin with a removable base, chill for 10 minutes. Line with nonstick paper, fill with uncooked rice and bake at 190°C/375°F/Gas 5 for 15 minutes. Remove rice and paper and bake for 5 minutes longer or until golden. Set aside to cool.

2. Heat 1 tablespoon oil in a frying pan over a medium heat, add onions and cook, stirring frequently, for 5 minutes or until soft. Using a slotted spoon remove from pan and cool. Add tomato slices to pan and cook for 5 minutes. Remove from pan and cool. Drain any juices from pan.

3. Heat remaining oil in pan, add zucchini slices and cook for 5 minutes or until soft. Remove from pan and cool.

4. Scatter onion over base of pastry case, sprinkle with thyme and black pepper to taste. Arrange tomato slices and zucchini slices, attractively, on top of onions, sprinkle with basil and parsley and black pepper to taste and bake for 15 minutes.

ingredients

> **1 sheet shortcrust pastry**
> **2 tablespoons olive oil**
> **2 onions, thinly sliced**
> **4 tomatoes, cut into thick slices**
> **4 zucchini, sliced**
> **2 teaspoons chopped fresh thyme or 1 teaspoon dried thyme**
> **freshly ground black pepper**
> **2 tablespoons finely chopped fresh basil**
> **2 tablespoons finely chopped fresh parsley**

....
Serves 6-8

tip from the chef

Serve this pie warm with a tossed green salad, crusty bread and a glass of dry white wine.

spiced
spinach pastries

■□□ I Cooking time: 25 minutes - Preparation time: 10 minutes

ingredients
> **375 g/12 oz puff pastry**
> **mango chutney**

spinach filling
> **2 teaspoons vegetable oil**
> **1 onion, chopped**
> **1 tablespoon black mustard seeds**
> **2 teaspoons curry paste**
> **10 large spinach leaves, chopped**
> **125 g/4 oz cottage cheese**
> **60 g/2 oz frozen peas**

method
1. To make filling, heat oil in a frying pan over a medium heat, add onion, mustard seeds and curry paste and cook, stirring, for 3 minutes or until onion is soft.
2. Add spinach to pan and cook for 8 minutes longer or until liquid from spinach evaporates. Stir in cottage cheese and peas. Remove pan from heat and set aside to cool.
3. Roll out pastry to 3 mm/$^1/_8$ in thick and using a 10 cm/4 in cutter, cut out rounds. Place a spoonful of filling in the center of each pastry round. Brush edges lightly with water, fold pastry over filling and press edges together to seal.
4. Place pastries on greased baking trays and bake at 180°C/350°F/Gas 4 for 12 minutes or until pastry is puffed and golden. Serve warm with mango chutney.

....
Makes 25

tip from the chef
Substitute any leftover cooked peas for the frozen quantity in this recipe. If fresh spinach is unavailable, frozen spinach, thawed and drained on absorbent kitchen paper, may be used instead.

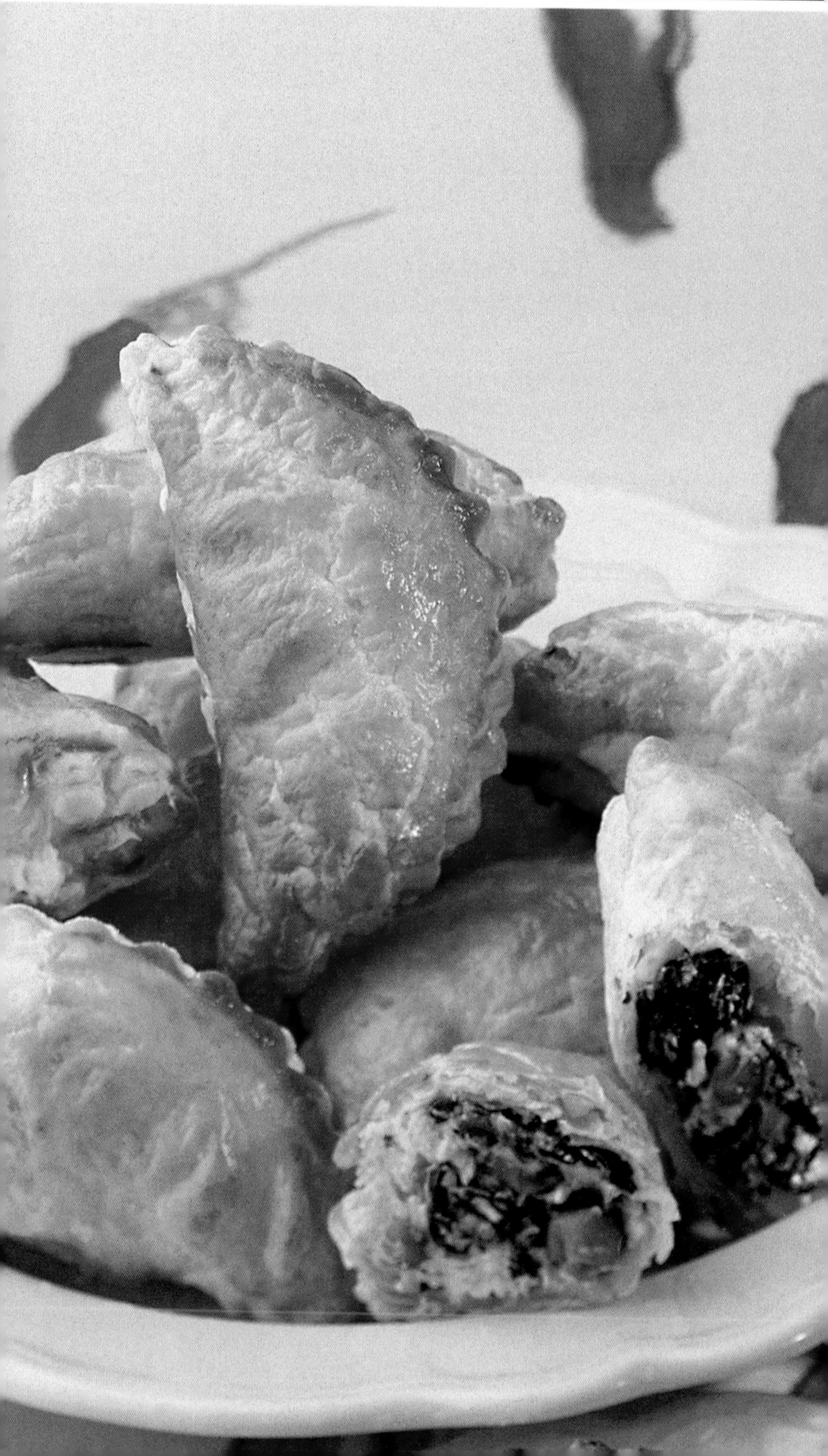

ricotta
and olive pie

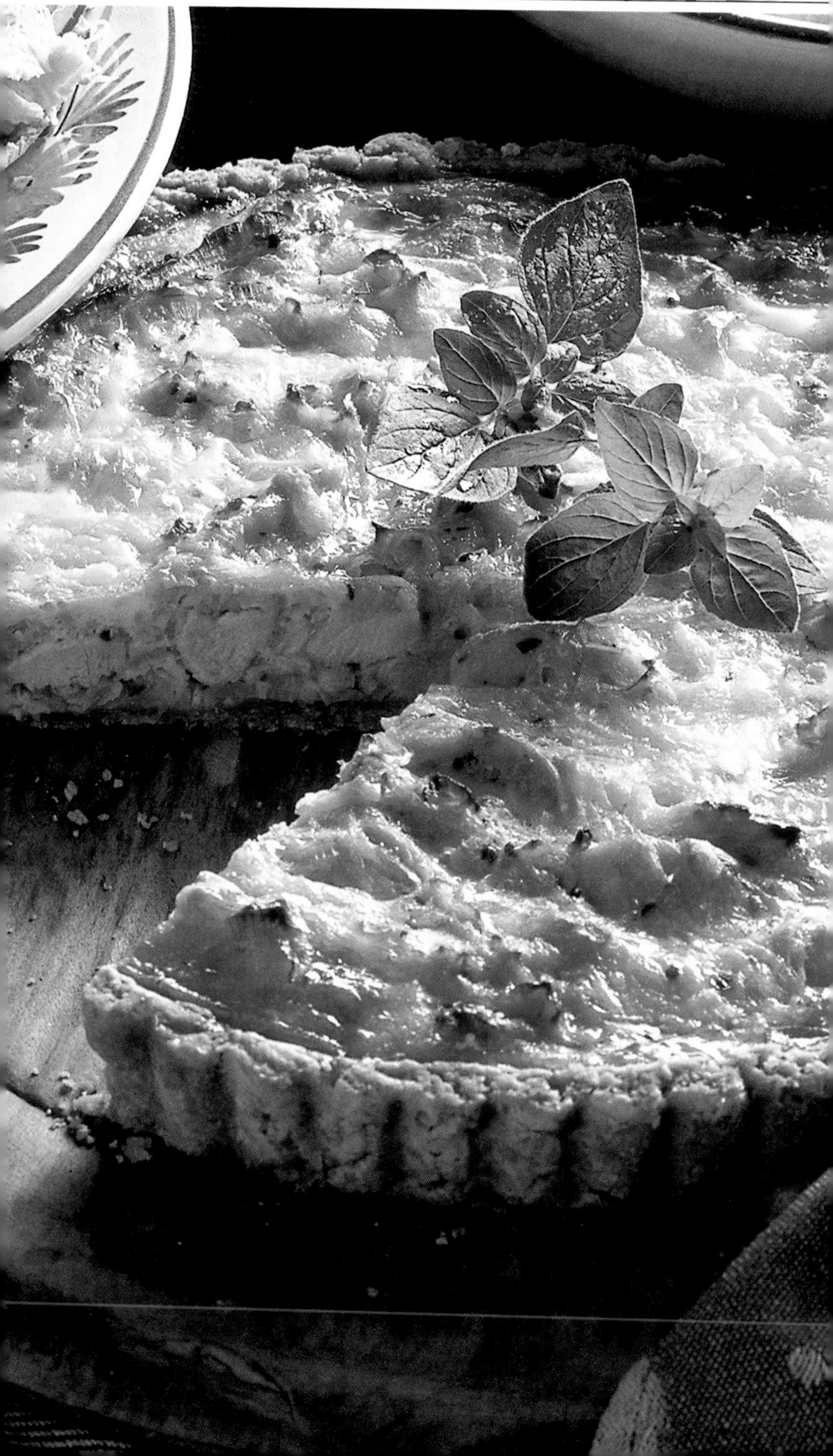

family meat pie

■ ■ ■ | Cooking time: 60 minutes - Preparation time: 20 minutes

method

1. To make filling, heat oil in a frying pan over a high heat and cook beef, in batches, turning frequently, for 5 minutes or until brown on all sides. Remove beef from pan and drain on absorbent kitchen paper.

2. Add onions and garlic to pan and cook over a medium heat, stirring, for 5 minutes or until golden. Add mushrooms and cook, stirring, for 3 minutes or until tender.

3. Return beef to pan and stir in parsley, stock, Worcestershire sauce and black pepper to taste. Bring to simmering and simmer, stirring occasionally, for 15 minutes or until meat is tender. Stir in cornflour and cook, stirring constantly, until mixture boils and thickens. Remove pan from heat and set aside to cool.

4. Spoon meat mixture into a 23 cm/9 in pie dish. Roll out pastry to 5 cm/2 in larger than pie dish. Cut a 2.5 cm/1 in strip from around the edge of pastry. Brush rim of pie dish with water and place pastry strip on dish rim. Place pastry circle over filling and pinch edges together to seal, then trim to neaten. Brush pastry with milk and using a sharp knife make three small slits in pastry. Bake at 220°C/425°F/Gas 7 for 15 minutes, reduce temperature to 190°C/375°F/Gas 5 and bake for 15 minutes longer or until pastry is puffed and golden.

Serves 4

ingredients

> **185 g/6 oz puff pastry**
> **1/4 cup/60 ml/2 fl oz milk**

beef and mushroom filling

> **1 tablespoon olive oil**
> **500 g/1 lb rump steak, cut into 2.5 cm/1 in cubes**
> **2 onions, thinly sliced**
> **1 clove garlic, crushed**
> **125 g/4 oz button mushrooms, sliced**
> **2 tablespoons chopped fresh parsley**
> **1/2 cup/125 ml/4 fl oz beef stock**
> **1 tablespoon Worcestershire sauce**
> **freshly ground black pepper**
> **1 tablespoon cornflour blended with 1 tablespoon water**

tip from the chef

The fat rating for this dish is high. However, compared to a traditional pie the fat content is reduced significantly. This allows you to enjoy this family favorite every once in a while. Serve it with lots of steamed green vegetables of your choice.

rainbow
vegetable terrine

■ ■ □ | Cooking time: 65 minutes - Preparation time: 15 minutes

ingredients

> **4 large eggplant, sliced
  lengthwise**
> **salt**
> **3 tablespoons olive oil**
> **200 g/6½ oz ricotta
  cheese, drained**
> **3 tablespoons chopped
  fresh basil**
> **freshly ground black
  pepper**
> **2 red peppers, roasted**
> **2 green peppers, roasted**
> **2 yellow peppers, roasted**

method

1. Place eggplant in a colander, sprinkle with
   salt and set aside to drain for 30 minutes.
   Rinse under cold running water, then pat
   dry with absorbent kitchen paper. Place
   on a baking tray, brush lightly with oil (a),
   and bake at 180°C/350°F/Gas 4 for
   20 minutes or until softened.
2. Place ricotta cheese, basil and black pepper
   to taste in a bowl and mix to combine.
3. Line base and sides of a 14 x 21 cm/
   5½ x 8½ in nonstick loaf tin with eggplant
   slices (b), allowing them to overhang
   the sides of tin by 5 cm/2 in.
4. Place a layer of red pepper in base of lined
   tin, then top with a layer ricotta mixture (c),
   a layer eggplant, a layer green pepper.
   Repeat layers using a different colored
   pepper each time until all ingredients are
   used. Fold overhanging eggplant over
   filling, cover with aluminum foil.
5. Bake for 45 minutes or until tender. Drain
   off any juices, cover with foil again, place
   a heavy weight on top and set aside
   for 1 hour. To serve, unmold and cut into
   thick slices.

tip from the chef

*To roast peppers, halve
and seed peppers
and place, skin side up,
under a preheated hot
grill. Cook until skin
blisters and chars, then
place in a paper
or plastic food bag, seal
and set aside until cool
enough to handle.
Remove from bag, peel
away skin.*

....
Serves 8

a   b   c

spinach
pasta loaf

■□□ I Cooking time: 50 minutes - Preparation time: 10 minutes

method

1. Cook pasta in boiling water in a large saucepan following packet directions. Drain and set aside.
2. Place eggs, cayenne pepper, sour cream, herbs, spinach, Gruyère cheese and pine nuts in a bowl and mix to combine. Mix in pasta.
3. Spoon mixture into a greased 11 x 21 cm/ 4 1/2 x 8 1/2 in loaf tin and bake at 180°C/350°F/Gas 4 for 40 minutes or until firm. Stand in tin for 5 minutes before turning out and serving.

ingredients

> 250 g/8 oz fettuccine
> 3 eggs, lightly beaten
> pinch cayenne pepper
> 1 cup/250 g/8 oz sour cream
> 6 tablespoons chopped fresh mixed herbs
> 1 bunch/500 g/1 lb English spinach, leaves blanched and chopped
> 125 g/4 oz Gruyère cheese, grated
> 90 g/3 oz pine nuts, toasted

....
Serves 4

tip from the chef

When purchasing pine nuts, look for a creamy-white color, as a grey color indicates rancidity. Store pine nuts, like all nuts and seeds, in a tightly closed container in the refrigerator to maintain freshness and flavor.

prosciutto
fettuccine mold

■□□ I Cooking time: 25 minutes - Preparation time: 15 minutes

ingredients

> 1 bunch English spinach, stems removed
> 250 g/8 oz spinach fettuccine
> 125 g/4 oz frozen minted peas
> 90 g/3 oz mushrooms, sliced
> 90 g/3 oz sun-dried peppers or tomatoes, sliced
> 30 g/1 oz Parmesan cheese, grated
> freshly ground black pepper
> 6 slices prosciutto or lean ham

method

1. Line a 20 cm/8 in soufflé dish with overlapping spinach leaves. Allow leaves to overhang dish by about 5 cm/2 in. Set aside.
2. Cook pasta in boiling water in a large saucepan following packet directions, drain well. Add peas, mushrooms, sun-dried peppers or tomatoes, Parmesan cheese and black pepper to taste to pasta and toss to combine.
3. Spoon half the pasta mixture into the spinach-lined dish, top with half the prosciutto or ham slices, then with remaining pasta mixture and prosciutto or ham. Fold spinach leaves over filling and cover dish with aluminum foil.
4. Place soufflé dish on a wire rack set in a baking dish. Half fill baking dish with hot water and bake at 180°C/350°F/Gas 4 for 15 minutes or until spinach is tender. Remove from oven and allow to stand for 10 minutes before turning out and slicing.

....
Serves 6

tip from the chef

Pasta is a wonderful food for the health-conscious, it is low in fat and high in complex carbohydrates.

polenta
and cheese loaf

■□□ | Cooking time: 40 minutes - Preparation time: 10 minutes

method

1. Place polenta and 1 cup/250 ml/8 fl oz stock in a saucepan and whisk until smooth. Place pan over a medium heat and gradually stir in remaining stock. Cook, stirring constantly, for 15-20 minutes or until polenta leaves side of pan. Stir in butter, Parmesan cheese and rosemary (a).

2. Spoon half the polenta mixture into a greased 11 x 21 cm/4$^1/_2$ x 8$^1/_2$ in loaf tin. Place red pepper strips lengthwise along one side of loaf and green pepper strips along the other side. Arrange goat's cheese (b) down the center.

3. Top with remaining polenta mixture (c) and press firmly with the back of a spoon. Bake at 180°C/350°F/Gas 4 for 20 minutes or until loaf is firm. Stand loaf in tin for 5 minutes before turning out.

ingredients

> **200 g/6$^1/_2$ oz polenta**
> **3 cups/750 ml/1$^1/_4$ pt vegetable stock**
> **30 g/1 oz butter**
> **60 g/2 oz Parmesan cheese, grated**
> **1 tablespoon chopped fresh rosemary or 1 teaspoon dried rosemary**
> **1 red pepper, roasted**
> **1 green pepper, roasted**
> **185 g/6 oz goat's cheese, crumbled**

tip from the chef

Serves 4

Serve this loaf with natural yogurt flavored with chopped fresh herbs. To roast peppers, see tip on page 40.

a

b

c

salmon,
rice and spinach loaf

■□□ I Cooking time: 50 minutes - Preparation time: 10 minutes

ingredients

> **9 spinach leaves, stalks removed**
> **450 g/15 oz canned salmon, drained and flaked**
> **3 eggs**
> **3 tablespoons sour cream**
> **2 tablespoons mayonnaise**
> **1 tablespoon lemon juice**
> **1/2 cup cooked rice**
> **2 tablespoons grated Parmesan cheese**

method

1. Boil, steam or microwave spinach leaves until soft.
2. Line the bottom and sides of a greased 22.5 x 12.5 cm/9 x 5 in loaf pan with half the spinach leaves, allowing some of the leaves to hang over the sides of the pan.
3. Squeeze excess moisture from remaining leaves. Chop and combine with all the remaining ingredients; season to taste.
4. Spoon salmon mixture into the spinach-lined dish. Enclose with the overhanging spinach leaves. Cover and bake at 190°C/375°F/Gas 5 for 45 minutes or until firm. Let stand for 10 minutes before serving.

....
Serves 4

tip from the chef

This loaf cooks quickly in the microwave. Remember to use a microwave-safe loaf dish, cover and cook on High (100%).

layered ham
and vegetable loaf

■■□ | Cooking time: 5 minutes - Preparation time: 15 minutes

method

1. Cut top from loaf and scoop out center leaving a 2 cm/3/4 in border. Reserve top of loaf. Reserve crumbs for another use.
2. Boil, steam or microwave spinach leaves until tender. Drain well and squeeze to remove as much moisture as possible.
3. Line base of loaf with a layer of spinach leaves. Then top with a layer each of ham, cheese, onion, tomatoes, sun-dried peppers or tomatoes, avocado and parsley. Repeat layers to use all ingredients.
4. Replace top of loaf, press down firmly and wrap tightly in plastic food wrap. Weigh down and chill for at least 1 hour.

....
Serves 6

ingredients

> **1 loaf wholemeal bread**
> **1 bunch English spinach**
> **185 g/6 oz lean ham, thinly sliced**
> **185 g/6 oz Cheddar cheese, thinly sliced**
> **1 red onion, thinly sliced**
> **2 large tomatoes, sliced**
> **90 g/3 oz sun-dried peppers or tomatoes**
> **1 large avocado, stoned, peeled and thinly sliced**
> **3 tablespoons chopped fresh parsley**

tip from the chef

The bread from the center of the loaf can be made into crumbs and used in another recipe. Allow the bread to dry out, then process in a food processor or blender. Crumbs can be stored in an airtight container for several days or frozen for longer storage.

bay and lime fish

■□□ | Cooking time: 10 minutes - Preparation time: 10 minutes

ingredients

> **6 small firm white fish fillets**
> **corn husks or aluminum foil**
> **12 slices lime**
> **12 fresh bay leaves**
> **1 fresh red chili, chopped**
> **freshly ground black pepper**

method

1. Place fish fillets in sweet corn husks or, if using aluminum foil, cut 6 pieces large enough to completely enclose the fillets, then place a fillet on each piece.
2. Top each fillet with 2 slices lime, 2 bay leaves and chili and black pepper to taste. Tie ends of husks or fold foil to encase fish.
3. Cook parcels on a preheated hot barbecue for 8 minutes or until fish flakes when tested with a fork.

....
Serves 6

tip from the chef
When buying fish fillets, look for those that are shiny and firm with a pleasant sea smell. Avoid fillets that are dull, soft, discolored or "ooze" water when touched.

chicken
with lentil purée

■ ■ ☐ | Cooking time: 30 minutes - Preparation time: 15 minutes

method

1. To make purée, bring a large saucepan of water to the boil. Add lentils, reduce heat and simmer for 15 minutes or until tender. Drain and set aside to cool slightly. Place lentils and stock in a food processor or blender and process until smooth.

2. Transfer purée to a saucepan, stir in garam marsala, cinnamon and black pepper to taste and cook over a medium heat, stirring, for 4 minutes or until purée thickens and is heated through. Set aside and keep warm.

3. Cook chicken, red and green peppers and zucchini on a preheated hot barbecue or under a grill, turning several times, for 10 minutes or until cooked and tender. Serve immediately with warm purée.

....
Serves 4

ingredients

> **2 boneless chicken breast fillets, halved lengthwise**
> **1 red pepper, quartered**
> **1 green pepper, quartered**
> **2 zucchini, halved lengthwise**

lentil purée

> **155 g/5 oz green lentils**
> **1 1/2 cups/375 ml/12 fl oz vegetable stock**
> **1 teaspoon garam masala**
> **1/2 teaspoon ground cinnamon**
> **freshly ground black pepper**

tip from the chef

Recent studies have shown that the fiber in legumes is soluble, and when eaten as part of a low-fat diet, helps to lower blood cholesterol levels and control the glucose levels of diabetics.

lamb
with oranges and rice

■ ■ ■ | Cooking time: 2 hours - Preparation time: 20 minutes

ingredients

> 1 kg/2 lb leg of lamb, trimmed of all visible fat
> 2 cloves garlic, thinly sliced
> 8 sprigs fresh lemon thyme or thyme
> 8 sprigs fresh rosemary
> freshly ground black pepper
> 4 oranges
> 1 cup/220 g/7 oz brown rice
> 1 cup/220 g/7 oz wild rice

method

1. Using a sharp knife make 8 small slits in surface of lamb. Fill each slit with a slice of garlic, a sprig of thyme and a sprig of rosemary and season to taste with black pepper.
2. Place lamb on a wire rack set in a baking dish, pour in 2.5 cm/1 in water and bake at 190°C/375°F/Gas 5 for 1 hour.
3. Place oranges on rack around meat and bake for 20 minutes longer or until oranges are tender and lamb is cooked to your liking.
4. Transfer lamb and oranges to a serving platter, set aside and keep warm. Skim fat from pan juices and reserve.
5. Cook brown rice and wild rice in boiling water for 40 minutes or until tender. Drain well, return to pan, stir in reserved juices and cook, stirring occasionally, for 5 minutes longer or until rice absorbs juices.
6. To serve, slice lamb and oranges, arrange attractively on serving plates and accompany with rice mixture.

....
Serves 6

tip from the chef

If blood oranges are available use these for a spectacular presentation. Blood oranges have reddish pink flesh.

lean roast

■■□ | Cooking time: 110 minutes - Preparation time: 20 minutes

method

1. To cook vegetables, place potatoes, pumpkin and sweet potato on a nonstick baking tray and bake at 190°C/375°F/Gas 5, turning once, for 1 hour or until vegetables are tender and golden.

2. Rub beef with garlic and black peppercorns and place on a wire rack set in a baking dish. Pour enough water into baking dish to come within 1 cm/1/2 in of the rack and bake for 40-45 minutes or until beef is cooked to your liking.

3. To make gravy, place instant gravy powder, water, wine and Worcestershire sauce in a small saucepan and cook over a medium heat, stirring constantly, until gravy thickens.

4. Slice meat and serve with roast vegetables and gravy.

ingredients

> **750 g/1 1/2 lb beef fillet**
> **2 cloves garlic, crushed**
> **2 teaspoons crushed black peppercorns**

roast vegetables
> **18 large potatoes, halved**
> **6 slices pumpkin**
> **6 pieces sweet potato**

gravy
> **2 tablespoons instant gravy powder**
> **1/2 cup/125 ml/4 fl oz water**
> **1/2 cup/125 ml/4 fl oz red wine**
> **1 tablespoon Worcestershire sauce**

....
Serves 6

tip from the chef

Add steamed green vegetables to this meal, if desired. Serve fresh fruit for dessert.

fruity
chicken casserole

■■□ | Cooking time: 35 minutes - Preparation time: 15 minutes

ingredients
> **12 chicken wings, rinsed and drained**
> **3 tablespoons flour**
> **3 tablespoons oil**
> **2 onions, sliced**
> **12 baby potatoes, scrubbed**
> **250 ml/8 fl oz chicken stock**
> **250 ml/8 fl oz apple juice or cider**
> **125 ml/4 fl oz lemon juice**
> **125 ml/4 fl oz honey**
> **220 g/7 oz dried apricots**
> **220 g/7 oz dried apples, chopped**
> **90 g/3 oz prunes, pitted**
> **12 black olives**
> **1 tablespoon chopped fresh lemon thyme**

method
1. Lightly coat chicken with flour. Heat oil in large saucepan, add chicken pieces and cook over medium heat for 8 minutes or until golden brown. Remove from pan and drain on absorbent kitchen paper.
2. Add onions and potatoes to pan, cook over low heat for about 5 minutes or until onion softens. Stir in stock, juices and honey.
3. Return chicken to pan, add apricots, apples and prunes. Bring mixture to the boil and simmer, covered, for 20 minutes or until chicken and fruits are tender.
4. Just before serving, stir in olives and thyme. Season to taste.

....
Serves 6

tip from the chef
This Middle Eastern inspired casserole looks great served on a bed of saffron rice and garnished with fresh thyme sprigs.

mixed
beans casserole

■ ■ □ | Cooking time: 110 minutes - Preparation time: 20 minutes

method

1. Place red kidney and black-eyed beans in a large bowl, cover with water and set aside to soak overnight. Drain. Bring a large saucepan of water to the boil, add beans and boil for 10 minutes. Reduce heat and simmer for 1 hour or until beans are tender. Drain and set aside.

2. Heat oil in a large saucepan over a medium heat, add garlic and onion and cook, stirring, for 3 minutes or until onion is soft and golden. Add tomatoes, cumin, mustard, golden syrup and tomato paste (purée) and bring to the boil. Reduce heat and simmer for 5 minutes.

3. Add cooked beans, carrots, zucchini, butter beans, broad beans and oregano to pan and simmer for 30 minutes or until vegetables are tender.

....
Serves 4

ingredients

- > 155 g/5 oz dried red kidney beans
- > 155 g/5 oz dried black-eyed beans
- > 1 tablespoon vegetable oil
- > 2 cloves garlic, crushed
- > 1 red onion, chopped
- > 440 g/14 oz canned tomatoes, undrained and mashed
- > 1 tablespoon ground cumin
- > 1 tablespoon dry mustard
- > 2 tablespoons golden syrup
- > 1 tablespoon tomato paste (purée)
- > 2 carrots, thickly sliced
- > 3 zucchini, thickly sliced
- > 440 g/14 oz canned butter beans, rinsed and drained
- > 100 g/3^{1}/2 oz shelled fresh or frozen broad beans
- > 2 tablespoons chopped fresh oregano or 1 teaspoon dried oregano

tip from the chef

All types of beans adapt to a huge range of seasonings. The beans in this casserole can be altered to accommodate whatever you have available. As an alternative, try a combination of haricot and butter beans with chickpeas, and substitute your favorite spices or dried herbs for the ground cumin and oregano.

index